Rufus Mufasa

Flashbacks & Flowers

Indigo Dreams Publishing

First Edition: Flashbacks & Flowers
First published in Great Britain in 2021 by:
Indigo Dreams Publishing
24, Forest Houses
Cookworthy Moor
Halwill
Beaworthy
Devon
EX21 5UU

www.indigodreams.co.uk

ISBN 978-1-912876-50-1

British Library Cataloguing in Publication Data. A CIP record for this book can be obtained from the British Library.

Designed and typeset in Palatino Linotype by Indigo Dreams.
Cover image by Becky Davies
www.beckydaviestheatredesigner-artist.com
Author photo by Noel Dacey
Printed and bound in Great Britain by 4edge Ltd.
Papers used by Indigo Dreams are recyclable products made from wood grown in sustainable forests following the guidance of the Forest Stewardship Council.

For Louise Richards,
my literary Fairy Godmother, who never let go of my hand
and for my daughters, who walked me home.

Acknowledgements

Y Gegin Fach – first published by Red Poets; *Church* – this poem features in a song I wrote entitled 'Walk around the 90's', written during my artist residency with People Speak Up; *Summer of '94, Candy Clouds, Saturday Skydiving Club, Llanelli, Trigger Warnings* – written during my artist residency with People Speak Up; *Bali Myna, In Loving Memory of Doll, Mr Iman, I Heard You Calling* – first published by Wrecking Ball Press, in 'I am both stranger and of this place'; *Uncle John* – commended in the 2018/19 Mother's Milk Books Poetry Prize; *Nanna's Hands* first published on-line by Young Poets Network in celebration of International Dylan Thomas Day; *Braiding Sweetgrass with Uncle John* – earlier version first published on-line in Good Dadhood Special Edition, 2017.

I would also like to thank the following: Anne Phillips, Becky Davies, Gareth Evans Jones, Harri Hertell, Hay Writers at Work, Hefin Karadog, Angela Karadog, Professor Lisa Lewis, Julia Williams, Julie Richards, Kristy Davies, Kultivera, Louise Walsh, Llwyd Owen, Makassar International Writers Festival, Mike Jenkins, Page Poetry Alive, People Speak Up, Peter Cox, Rhys Mwyn, The British Arts Council and Tŷ Newydd.

Flashbacks & Flowers is Rufus Mufasa's debut collection.

The development of this collection was funded by a Literature Wales Writer's Bursary, supported by the National Lottery through the Arts Council of Wales.

CONTENTS

Flashbacks & Flowers

Every family has its scribe
January 2019

Last night I dreamed I was with Auntie Phyllis
and Uncle John – in Uncle Gwyn's house, all 3 of us
sat on the same armchair – Uncle Gwyn's
or mine when I'd visit... and we
frantically trying to work out how I was
going to catch my flight to L.A with
only 40 minutes to get to London from
Penybanc – without a passport in my hand
and a bad connection to the taxi line...
but we were all hopeful I'd make it.

Swings & Roundabouts

1

This is my Moose Hall memory
badge boasting five
white top, navy culottes
big girl, my mother (g)listening.

Matching belt
I couldn't master the clasp
a ying-yang kind of clip
my fingers didn't have the knack.

Black velvet shoes made for tapping
all over over-stained blocks
some rocked, some missing
silverfish sanctuary.

Dee's satin dress
abstract astronaut home job.
Neil smashed Superman
Skeletor visits with a smoke machine.

I left it too late to get to the toilet

bleached
cold
stern.

My mother got there in time to silence my cries
held my one hand, navy culottes in the other
under a thunderstorm that made truth impossible
but her navy-blue eyes say he's been,

but not to dance.

2

We found a flat on Church Street
lived on eggs, beans and bread
paid weekly for meter squared carpet.

We left him with his beige tiles
shards of glass his legacy
silverfish for friends.

Big bells always chimed
in and out of time
with our new lives.

Not fully poor Viennetta
scooping confetti from concrete cracks
for Orangina SuperTed Magic bottle banks.

3

Rainbow stained front door
gold cherub knocker not needed
Grandfather clock greeting.

This sweetshop my new neighbour
classy crystal jars, caramel counter
cola bottles that took full hours to devour.

Redundant gold scales bowl
dusty wizard like weights

and I still stole.

4

The new neighbours' lounge, long and round
Kash Koolidge windows
supersized sash universe a backdrop.

Mahogany bureau
its chair my throne
Art Deco Quink ink
silver-fountain-pen fairy wand

and I'd write my name over and over
in a leather spell book
drawing dogs, cats, kisses, hearts

in charge of sticking stamps
first and second class
watching-wild-flowers-waltz.

The walls, made of sideboards having a cwtch
some long, some tall, some strange, all stunning
dressed in enough china for ten tea parties.

A scent with a constant sense of Christmas
misty marzipan, itchy icing, sherry trifle,
cider; Mr Walrus – clear view of my play –

his suit, redundant
his stick, slightly politer than bossy
his eyes wide, but half there –

a watery film between us.

His clean had a funny whisper
his rickety a sporadic skip
and we'd crawl up Maple Mountain

take twelve steps to Hickory Dock
I'd step in when he shook
or if he needed my skeleton keys.

Then, with my hand in his
we'd ride waves
chiming; ding-dong-gong howling

as every bone played its own beat.
I once lost a tooth
learning to bend space and time.

5

My mother screamed
put my blotches in her bed

called The Doctor, home visit
German measles, he said.

He forgot his gold pen
I'd have given it back.

Dadi was allowed to visit
we held hands in the day's dark.

He brought books and biscuits
re-checked my brow for change

spilt Lucozade over my fever
so a piece of him could stay.

6

In the dark dampness of that flat
me and Mami danced.
We welcomed in the age of hip hop
the Fat Boys taught me beatbox and rap.

We believed Yazz whole-heartedly
that *The Only Way is Up.*
We knew all about Chapman's *Fast Cars*
but I was never the *Groovy Kind of Love.*

Teardrops meant different things to us,
Tell it to my heart did too.
I beg my sentimental soul *Don't Believe The Hype*
but I loved learning to dance with you.

7

We Moved
like pieces of furniture
Mami made new vows

I was not invited
to their time in the sun
with red & white roses.

We watched on VHS
The waves kissing their feet
Calypso drums played.

Maybe that's why
I loved Harry Belafonte
made Him my new God

later changed my name
because I could no longer be
called Ruthie.

Maybe I'll be as brave
to trust caregivers with you
when you revert to childhood

and I'll pack up your things
then maybe I can
move on...

Blue banger beach rides with Uncle Danny

Auntie Jackie throat croaky and busty
Whipped ninety-nines – I'd eat their flakes and mine.

Low tide cuttlefish quest, schools of rock pools
Springer-Spaniel best-buddy Welsh-Whisky
Blue banger beach rides with Uncle Danny.

Paw-printing shamans, wet sands our notepad
Tap-dancing waves, tease-tame freedom-in-chains
Whipped ninety-nines – I'd eat their flakes and mine.

Phone calls from Mami Wata and Mermaids
Brackish cabalistic vinegar chips
Blue banger beach rides with Uncle Danny.

Homeward rock-a-bye windows open wide
The wrong kind of incense to learn to like
Whipped ninety-nines – I'd eat their flakes and mine.

Cwtched-up daydreaming – damp dog my blanket
Supremes and Stevie Wonder lullabies
Blue banger beach rides with Uncle Danny
Whipped ninety-nines – I'd eat their flakes and mine.

Y Gegin Fach

Onyx framed fire, furious amber dancers leaking blood blue.
Cwtch dan stâr, the home to everything you need and don't.
Papur wal retro made of lung-like flowers
every shade of oranges and lemons.

Cadair ffyddlon Auntie Phyllis
yn croesawu hi nôl pob nos Wener.
Clincian y llwy yn erbyn y gwydr, basn llawn bara-the.
Her only other habit Coronation Street.

Y bwrdd cadarn, caer – our fortress made of blankets
Uncle John our little boy
pack of Players, Snap, 21, Solitaire, Patience, pens, papur
"Duw, you've got beautiful handwriting, Ruthie."

Old gas cooker, chip pan filled with sâm
a big bosh that both of them used.
Huge concrete steps down to the long lands
where we'd learn growing, burning, seasons, soul.

School Reports

Nursery

Mrs P, really liked me;
I carry your nature/object table still.
Years later I rescued your dog from two builders that had tied him up, thinking he wasn't spoken for...

Mrs A, infants, big, thick, raven-black wavy hair
with a matching tone
with a depth I'd get lost in.
I thought she was the coolest most beautifullest woman
this double denim Queen...

Mrs J1, auburn tint,
used to let me sleep at my desk,
let me grate up all the orange crayons like carrots, playing house...

Mrs E, half lady, half white owl,
had one blue eye, one brown
and played the piano like the thunder god Thor.
She let me build Lego.
I once built a huge house, but not huge enough
so I imagined inventing a machine that could zap it bigger
to move in to...

Mrs J2, the headmistress
red-tailed hawk with a hint of Art-Deco dragon.
Her powerful pitch made AR cry for his mother on our first day
and she was always smoking
walking in and out of classes
in her office
glamorously dressed in red, huge phone to her left, always smoking...

Juniors

Mrs D,
half sparrow half hamster
gave me chords and choir
at the piano like a sergeant major
daily mantras
Cymraeg y ddaear…

Mrs H,
you were catalyst to the rap
taught me to chant times tables.
Had this funny habit of putting the arm of your glasses in the corner of your mouth
which left you with a scar running down the side of your chin,
left side I think
and I really liked you, but one day you broke my heart
because I used red pen to do my work, just like you
but you shrieked when you saw it
said red is only for teachers
and made me do it all again, in blue...
Actually, you broke my heart a second time
thought I hadn't finished my project
that I'd spent weeks on.
It was about cars
and it was beautiful
I'd copied all the classics, old and new
and wrote a story about my father, who was once a Raleigh driver
but that day, I had forgotten it
I was probably between houses
the only child in my class whose parents lived separately...
I still have the wooden keyring of my initial that your husband made for your class
it sits on my cuckoo clock...

Miss J3,
even with big nostrils I still though you were lush
motherly cwtchy look with a tomboyish charm.
You were sometimes short with me
like the time I broke my wrist on the yard at playtime and
nobody told you I'd left
like it was my fault
but you really taught me how to sing
I fell in love with Welsh more, through song
and you meant every note you belted out
trance-like goofy features.
You lost a baby.
I didn't quite understand
but I ached for you...

Mr J,
wasn't technically my teacher, but I loved him.
I really loved him.
And he'd stand with me at first play
let me take a bite of his apple and share his coffee
and let me play cricket with the boys.
I once accidentally smashed DB in the face with a bat but didn't
get in trouble...

Miss P,
taught us briefly while Miss J3 was off.
I thought she was everything, wearing men's waistcoats
and how she danced into the piano
how she conducted us
how we could read her
how her eyes said everything
but I don't think she ever saw me
she had her favourites
but on a trip in the last year
(the trip I snogged SR and he tasted of strawberry sweets and

gave me his Adidas jumper)
on that trip I sang *My Brother* in the show on the last night
and Miss P saw me
our eyes locked
and she asked me to sing it at the concert back at school
and my father came along
he didn't tell me I was good
just said that it was his song
I'd stolen it from his show
the one where he'd dress up as a little boy
I thought he was amazing
even though he came in late and finished too soon
but that doesn't matter
nobody else would know
but I did
because his every show I was front row...

Mrs J4,
tiny thing, soft and stern
Brewer's blackbird bob
I never knew where we stood
but she did lots of reading
(I especially digged *The Turbulent Term of Tyke Tyler*)
and in her class I remember two student teachers, from the North...
The one was named Teleri, a beautiful blonde spoodle
and she'd chat to me like real
I still have a photo of us
and I remember thinking what a great teacher she'll be...
The other one, red-billed firefinch
and she said Salvador Dali sooo funny
and I loved her for bringing this man to my table...

Mr W,
I liked you for a while
I once wrote a story about Santes Dwynwen

and you were invited to my class to come and read it...
You'd walk up and down the aisle in assembly
with your huge shovel like hands down the back of your pants
and it was a lucky day if you got chosen to operate
the overhead projector
or to help Miss turn her music sheets at the piano...
You'd teach us the recorder but liked the sound of yours too much...
I once had to try a summer dress on in your office while you
were in the room.
Something kicked off between us girls one day:
it was all a bit silly
and SB told tales on me
and you marched me to your office and made me stand alone
outside your door all afternoon
and I cried.
I cried so loudly I echoed in every corridor
and my new next-door neighbour came to the school
for her children
and I told her "I don't belong here, please help me.
Get me out of here, get me home,"
and she challenged Mr W
but he just shouted in my face
in front of her
saying I was a bad girl
saying my tears are an act
and I couldn't stop sobbing
and my new neighbour walked away without me
and I had to wait until the bell
that was above my head, and when it rang it broke me into a
thousand pieces...
at least she chose another school for her children.
Neither of us told my mother.

I wish we had…

Summer of '94

1

I still play with dolls
on the low like
But I already wear a bra
on the low like…

My cousin Ferret has huge boobs
and two children, Hamster, and Mouse.
I'll spend most of the summer
make-believing at their house.

Their Dad, Eagle, is out of shape,
rules the roost none the less.
He raises his voice regular, I don't mind
It's less frightening than my Dadi's silence.

Ferret trusts me with her babies
I sing them to sleep and am waiting when they wake.
The sun shines bright this summer
we walk miles together everyday.

From the red brick row of council houses on the hill
through country lanes and windy back roads
Hamster on my back, his arms tightly wrapped
Mouse sat sunny in her mobile throne.

Passing cottages and bungalows,
phone boxes, wild blackberry bushes.
Legend has it, this is the lost lands,
a base for broken women who've been banished.

Widows, well that's one thing.
Witches is another.
But some of these women
chose to leave husbands, find new lovers.

And they can sustain themselves
they grow roses, have ponds full of frogs
and their homes are as beautiful as their gardens
they live alongside wildlife, cats and dogs.

And they were always smiling,
offering me and my babies milk and cake.
Said I was a good Mami
but blessed us to make sure we got home safe.

And when we got home we all had tea.
I kiss my babies goodnight, bless their sleep.
The King of the Castle sits in his cheap,
blue velvet throne, in charge of the TV.

But Ferret tells him it's my turn now
and I always choose my favourite movie.
This small victory is huge, cos I get to see my Johnny
Dirty Dancing, but I could never be Baby.

My boobs are already bigger than hers.
My hair got real dark
but I'm so glad I get to watch this
even if I don't yet quite get some parts.

This is the best summer ever:
playing big girl, playing house,
longing for my Johnny to show up and love me
as much as I love Hamster and Mouse.

2

On those walks we met Cat Lady
She seemed younger than the rest.
Not Crazy Cat Lady like the drama teacher I'll soon get
This was a feline-flex beyond finesse.

This pint-sized Cleopatra
Worshipped the Moon and the Sun
Dark, delicate, doll-like features
But her arms were made of guns.

Her chest was tiny, but she oozed sexuality
She dripped in sureness and in-control femininity
She left behind a mansion, there's different levels to happy, clearly
Or maybe age doesn't exclude the longing of finding your Johnny.

Others would rather you did this on the low
Refrain from putting freedom centre-stage
But Cat Lady drove the biggest bright red Mazda
With pride, her head held high, rejected their shame.

And she could survive on the sun, and fancy French breakfasts
That sometimes lasted from sunrise into midday
She wore war-paint like the ancients
And learnt that her body wasn't a house for men's pain.

We are pre-Britney Spears
But she's *Hit Me Baby One More Time*, and a teacher
She sings *You Want a Piece of Me?*
Middle fingers up to the haters.

Our shared story doesn't go to plan
But here, right now, she shows me womanhood, Europe, the sun.
But, much later on in my journey, this summer will remind me
How to totally fuckin' boss it

when learning to leave a man.

Candy Clouds, Saturday Skydiving Club

Too young to fly I photo my father
Eyeing up his navy Raleigh jacket.

Wished and waited, not mine to inherit
Later I'd claim a bad boy's Adidas
Candy Clouds, Saturday Skydiving Club.

I'd forage the lands for lost property
Knew the drills 1-2-3 check canopy
Eyeing up his navy Raleigh jacket.

Can't keep that poor boy down theme tune blasting
Formation, murmuration mastering
Candy Clouds, Saturday Skydiving Club.

Dedicated, I still got downgraded
New girls, new issues contaminated
Eyeing up his navy Raleigh jacket.

Prayed to every green blade, DJ'd his tapes
Wrong way around relationship instincts
Candy Clouds, Saturday Skydiving Club
Eyeing up his navy Raleigh Jacket.

Church

I can't take my eyes off the man from Ghana
His brown suit and shoes
white shirt, white handkerchief in
each held high hand.

I can't take my eyes off the man from Ghana
the way he doesn't need sight to see
doesn't need to see to dance
the way he sees me
with his eyes closed.

I can't take my eyes off the man from Ghana
who takes the tambourine from my hands
who takes my hand in his
who chants in tongues
far better than Pastor Miles.

I can't take my eyes off the man from Ghana
whose name I do not know
but he knows mine
gifts me a new one
so I become two
we become one in the dance.

He gifted me in(sight) and chant
gave me a new drum
which our legs move to
synchronised without warning
stored inside forever
so my hips will know
how to walk the wild way home...

Comp

Saturday morning. I try my uniform on to find that my feet have grown.
I can tell that the shoe shop guy and my father do business: it's all winks and smiles, but no Kickers.
If this had happened on Mami's watch I'd be having Kickers. She once bought me a lilac suede pair of Kicker boots and I loved them so much I wore them to bed and to do PE. I wore them with everything. But Mami's not here, and I walk out of the shop, my pair of chunky, rough as guts shoe shop dregs boxed and bagged.
Monday morning. I am up and dressed, surprisingly excited. My cousin T lives near my Dad's and will pick me up and walk with me. She's two years older. I like her. Her mother is a militant clean-freak cow, who has been nice on the odd occasion, but will much later on in this story say lies about me meeting boys.
My father's not that bothered, doing his s l o w m o t ioned shaving, following his s l o w m o t ioned bathing, wearing a white vest, and a blue towel like a skirt. I present myself to him in my uniform, the longest my skirt will ever be, and I say "Hey Dad, watch this," and sing the song like Pinocchio when he's doing the puppet show before he becomes a real boy, and I rub my black shoes on the back of my fresh snow-white socks, and he just looks so disgusted, tells me I'm stupid, that I'll ruin my socks, and I can't wait for that knock on the front door, to save me from this. The unknown has got to be better...
And T, her hair like the sun, this kind canary, her paleness so pleasant, and we walk, so normal, and she doesn't say a word about my Mami, and I'm glad, and she's kind, and funny without trying, and I'm glad she's my cousin, and a bigger girl in my new school. Years later she'll go out with my ex-boyfriend, and later still she'll marry the boy from nursery who cried for his mother when I told him to stop picking his nose or he'll turn into a witch, and I got told off but said "It's true, my

mother said, and she doesn't lie". I'll later work with this boy in Swansea, before he ever thinks about marrying T, and we blast Shania Twain in his mother's car driving over the mountain. I liked him. Him and his mother were Beavers.
But today, I need T. One day, I'd like to thank her...
The pavements are busy, armies in green, all heading the same way, and before getting there they stop off for sweets, swelling inside buildings picking up bags of sugar. I can't quite believe this world, and I'm in it now...
By the time the bell cried for the last time we are all in. I'm in a huge hall, but the school's smallest, deep brown patchwork beneath my feet, stood in these hellish ugly shoes, surrounded by new faces, and faces I see at weekends, kids from schools all over these Valleys, merging.
It's wild and amplified. Our spirit animals dance and howl above us, the high ceiling of this dated hall trying to contain them. And that's when I see her, NC, the most beautiful boy-looking girl, tall and sure, piercing cat eyes, three colours like mine, full short hair, tonal wild waves, and we are wearing the exact same shoes. We don't say that out-loud, but I will love her forever, and she won't let anyone fuck with me, for a long while at least.
Mr P commands the altar-like school hall stage and the instant silence almost took me out. Mr P will later scream at me in a hall full of the entire lower school about not having the correct jumper on, and I'll explain it's because I'm going on a skiing trip, then he says "I'll see you in my office after assembly," and it's me and BJ getting screamed at (BJ's used to getting screamed at), BJ made the same mistake as me, and Mr P insists on taking us home to get changed and I cry and cry, and it's to BJ's house first, and it's just me and Mr P in the car, and I cry and cry some more and he says he's changed his mind about taking me home and I'm to tell BJ that I've just remembered that my Mother is out, and BJ gets back in the car, changed, looks at me, wonders what's happened, and Mr P takes me to my class, Drama, Mrs P, and she too tells me no more crying, thrown into

class, I'm sat next to Mr P's daughter, she gives me evils, says I really should stop crying. I wonder if she really knows?
But today, my first day, I have the right jumper on.
Mr P splits us into our classes.
The A's, who we'll later learn are not getting A's, and need extra help. There's a few helpers here from my old school, moving up with the kids they help, and they're all going to this class. My cousin T told me that in the old days, the class forms had two letters, and the A's used to be called MT, but they changed it cos MT makes the word "empty" – "Like their heads, init." But A's is a bit awkward too, why not put them in the middle of the alphabet, subtle like.
7A
7B
7C
7D
7E
7G
7L
7M
7S
7W
None of us really know what the letters mean. I'm 7W. There are mainly English forms, but three Welsh ones. My form teacher is beautiful. I've never seen such a small adult before. She looks so fragile. Not unhealthy, not skinny, just so tiny. She wore her hair like a head dress, tight bouncy, thick, long, shining auburn red hair that fell into a perfect narrowing as it reached the base of her back. I didn't fancy her, she was just spellbindingly beautiful and made me believe in the women from the Mabinogion.
There's a girl called CNake in my class. I've seen her on the weekends in Ragnant when visiting my family. She's been nasty to me in the Raven Park. (There is a magic tree in this park, and many moons later I will find a way into the tree and it will take me all the way to the Egyptian Pyramids. But that

part of the journey is too confusing right now). But CNake's trying to act all cool now. She'll be back to being a bitch soon enough. And there's Costella, who I've met on the weekly Welsh classes we attended at Comp before the summer holidays, and I like her, she seems so grown up, sporty but with a make-up vibe, and all the boys fancy her, but even aged eleven she knows she's better than them.
GG is the 7W's class hotty. He's way more rough and ready than Paul Pixie, the class hottie I've had for the last four years of primary, and he ain't even all that. I remember him showing me his willie in Mr's E's class in infants. I was never into him, maybe once, a little, but it made me sick how all the teachers swooned over him, and he got chosen for everything, all the singing, all the sports, the boy could even draw. He once drew a gypsy cart, I mean mine was pretty impressive, but his was next level... but here, in this next level new world, he's in a different class, the other Welsh form, and I hear he's got stiff competition. There's a new boy in the line-up, WolfLion, big, strong, blonde, even blonder than Paul Pixie, who overnight has been reduced to a mousy muddy blonde in comparison, and even though WolfLion's teeth ain't quite as straight as Paul Pixie's, it kind of adds to 'the look'. And apparently he's better than Paul Pixie at rugby, and they'll spend the next five years competing.
GG wins our class hands down. There's EagleOwl, who's got a symmetrical sweet face, cute curtains, but he's no GG. The other possibility is GW, Man United mad, and he's been at the top of the league table all summer in the Raven Park, and at his old school, but it doesn't matter how much gel he has on his curtains, or how on trend his coat is, underneath his trousers he's got sparrow legs and bandy knees, I saw them in the summer, and he does this weird squealing thing that really doesn't sound right. I'll snog them all.

Auntie Shirley

My Mami sometimes called me Sweet Pea
Other elders called me Ruthie
My Irish cousins called me Rufus
My Auntie Shirley called me her Chirpy-Cheeky-Chickadee.

I didn't know that Chickadees were birds then
But I did know that she loved them
Especially the little ones
Like Hummingbirds, Blue Tits and Sparrows.

I though her favourites
Would be Owls
Because she was one
Blonde, classy, slim and symmetrical.

She said I was Lion
Helped me find my roar
She's still with me every time I bathe
Saying "dry between your toes"

"Buy yourself flowers."
Yellow Roses were her favourite
And she'd look in her Bible
If she needed help with some answers

"Other answers will be in the sky,
Or deep inside you."
And her favourite song to sing was
Wherever I lay my hat, that's my home.

One day I asked her if Chief Joseph was her father.
Thought she might be confused, or cross, but she just smiled.
She knew exactly what I meant
Explained that he's my special guide Earthside.

She taught me that Angels are gold
Lavender was Jesus
She was gas-lit for months
Before the January diagnosis.

Mami was worried
About us seeing her with no hair
On the way to her house
I picked up an Easter egg.

And she was so proud of her wigs
So relieved to be believed
But it was so hot that June
She was 47, I was 13.

I've never seen my Mami sob like that,
Except once, at Christmas,
When Dadi kept my sister
That time.

But Auntie Shirley taught me
That there's no death,
Only
A change of worlds

And she's singing
Wherever I lay my hat,
In the sky, by my side,
In my magic mind's eye...

Rita

She never held me as a baby
Never made me any shawls.

I'd heard "stuff" but didn't dare ask questions.
To Dadi she was dead.

I'm 7, in the school hall
Choir practice, Mrs D
Singing *Mamgu Bach Annwyl*
And I cry, proper sob
For this missing link.

Mrs D dives in with tissues and cwtches
Tells me Mamgu would surely be in heaven
And I stop her with an outpour of information I didn't even
Realise I knew.

Rita wasn't dead
She'd been banished
Dadi cut all ties at 15
But I knew she'd left that nervous twitch.

Mrs D told my Mami
Mami talked to me
Next thing we'd arranged tea.

I knew her face
Her hair was mine
Her smile said she'd sent for me
Never claimed to be guilt free
And I knew she was complex from the get-go.

The Elders found out about our secret meetings
Told me never ever to say.
Dadi didn't mention it
But Dadi made me pay.

Rita told me unspeakables about my tribe,
Taught me spells I must never pen,
Gifted me trunks of earrings,
Chests full of silk crowns,
Told me men would try to steal my powers,
That they'd see my transitions arrive way before I.

And I'd wear the earrings
And the crowns,
Defiant and daring
Waiting to be scolded

By The Elders, by the teachers,
By my Dadi.
But they were either invisible to their eyes
Or had no choice but to allow it.

Rita taught me tarot, star maps, invasion, hexing
Similar to the women Dadi visited
Who told me I was just like them, too.
Dadi liked witches and needed a mother.
I'd become both.

I got too powerful for Dadi.
I even used his blades when it was time
I turned 15 and tipped transitions.

Transgenerational karma has a bittersweet taste.

Once Were CaeCoedians

I can't shift the stench of TCP.
Deena Dumps was going to kill me. The bullying bitch had back up and the security of a few extra stone, alcohol logic enhancing her jealous jibes. Her Pit Bull probed, "Don't you have a home to go to? Doesn't your mother know where you are?"
Ratty said she didn't want trouble and was friends with us both. The peace pipe filled the room, but it wasn't enough. Deena Dumps and her cronies ran these streets, and my face didn't fit. B said I should leave. My assassins congregated in the room next door. I was no longer safe in the safe house. I picked up my pride and put on my platforms. I had a fur coat that my best friend Jade had lent me for the funeral. It was my shield, but I doubt it could withstand a kick-in. B offered me a drink and his hand. He said he'd get me home safely. I walked past my enemies, with B, so that they could see I had somebody on my side.
The January air hit me and the frosty fog pinched. I'd not drunk enough to warrant being this distorted. I was familiar with the route. I'd walked it many times, even when wonky, but we were heading towards Troll Bridge. I avoided it at dark, and tonight it's inky-black. It was the perfect shortcut when light. I don't think the bridge had a bad reputation, more so my imagination, and if I ever did use that route in the dark I'd pelt it up the narrow steep hill through to the top gate, back to the safety of street lamps. The gothic gate was so corroded it leaked orange slime, so you'd have to boot it to avoid contamination.
I had no reason to fear Troll Bridge that evening. B was heavy-duty and five years my senior. I felt somewhat antagonistic, defiant, as childish as that sounds. I dared the Trolls, taunted them, but they didn't show.
We were safe, through the gate. My house was further than B's. I said I could get myself home now, thank you, but he was decoying me towards his, a path off a path that was unfamiliar, into a silent grey house. I resisted. I fell. Grazed knees, hurt

head, sound silenced.
Time passed.
I woke up, gasping for breath, dehydrated, no clothes. The bed felt so high, like in the Princess and the Pea. I was in the land of giants. I'd have to jump. I sensed a body next to me, but was too petrified to look.
I was down. Found my black trousers, no knickers, but I got everything else on, quietly, quickly, but my struggle with my platforms stirred him, and peering down he said he liked them. Failed armour on, I felt for the door, blinded by fear, stumbled down steep stairs, wondering how I got up them. He threw down keys.
I ran to a phone box, called my frenzied mother, it was 5.30am didn't I know? I apologised. She said she's buried me ten times in her mind.
I ran home. She was so angry she ignored me getting in. She barged into my room at 7:30am and said I was going to school. I didn't argue. I dressed my sores and blisters the best I knew how, inside and out. First lesson was double maths.
He later married my best friend, Jade. They have a girl. She attends the same High School where her mother and I met.
I got a D maths G.C.S.E.
I can't shift the stench of TCP.

Weasel

At fifteen I wanted to devour you[1].
I rocked up to your brother's suicide
with roses I'm yet to receive.

Ten red, ten white.
Your Auntie Julie answered,
mixed messages in her smile.

The co-dependency we'd learn,
the sunsets & lies we'd normalise,
the sorries we'd say with our bodies.

There wasn't a vase big enough
for this impulsive love-lust
disguised in/as condolences.

You told me you took them
to his fresh gave –
the only offering you made to his memory.

Then you drank yourself selfless
to silence your demons
and the ones you'd inherited from him.

---

[1] Tishani Doshi

Tina, the Staffordshire Bull Terrier

Brindle beauty, hench and a happenin';
I remember the 5th of November.

Brown leather studded collar, silver chains,
Gangsta' steps, a baller's beat, aged 13;
Tina, the Staffordshire Bull Terrier.

You'd sometimes piss on my side of the bed,
Keep me in check, upset, you were here first;
I remember the 5th of November.

Lady Di class with a Kat Slater side,
Working Bando's Jessica Rabbit slide;
Tina, the Staffordshire Bull Terrier.

Pride stride negotiating tick and cones;
You tried to get in the washing machine –
I remember the 5th of November.

The both of us hiding under the stairs,
Made vows and howled, held you like my lost child.
Tina, the Staffordshire Bull Terrier,
I remember the 5th of November.

Da'Cu

Not a man of many words
but his heart was as big
as the p a u s e s he took
during those conversations
that adults should not have
with little ears locked in rooms.

S l o w m o t i o n e d M a n
Thai Chi style
genuine kindness
love filled eyes…

He fell in the bath
and rather than say
he needed our help
said he fancied a change.

Chemo stole his pride and words
everyone used theirs
like he was no longer there
in the room that was his.

I'd read the rolls of his eyes
that screamed "they are pushing their luck"
we p r o l o n g e d h i s p a i n
with our failure to face facts.

Millennial Borders

My borderline Cockett/Townhill make-shift
Home for now, schooling some things I don't want
No more Mumbles, it belongs to childhood.

Telecommunications industry
Buildings of businessmen, steroids and speed
My borderline Cockett/Townhill make-shift.

The Palace, class A's – back then I danced Rave
Escape DJ's salaried alongside
No more Mumbles, it belongs to childhood.

Top Banana to avoid the Come Down
Dai Flies swiped my Purple Haze down The Dunes
My borderline Cockett/Townhill make-shift.

Chav meets David Evans and Habitat
Bong Shops every corner, Mix for super
No more Mumbles, it belongs to childhood.

Clutch control free-riding blue Fiesta
Every pay-day sale-rail, party bigger
My borderline Cockett/Townhill make-shift
No more Mumbles, it belongs to childhood.

215 Forest Hall

1

Michael was a Nigerian Prince
I did and didn't believe this
but he had ten rows of Tims
and just as many Marlboro Light cartons
and just as much fresh ocean blue denim.

Michael denied loving Mary J Blige
but always danced with me anyway
laughed all the way through *No More Drama*
but knew every word.

Michael loved my hair
despite it being a timeline of trauma
and he'd knead it singing Mufasaaa
while I chain smoked, sending prayers to the heavens.

His hands so gently present,
preparing my scalp
for the tightness, for the order.

Michael had beautiful lips
that I never kissed,
but there were many times he held me,
like he knew so much more than I could ever say.

I was running when I met Michael,
no ACES or metoo then.
I was fighting for my life when I met Michael,
and he upgraded my pen.

He called me Queen, he call me Mufasaaaa,
there wasn't a person on my block that didn't know my name.
Michael, if you're reading this,
you are the best King.

2

Ramla looked straight out of Ancient Egypt.
We wore matching dungarees;
we'd dance to *Peaches and Cream* on repeat
like Gangsta Gods.

We'd make up our own diction for words:
Balcony became BalaConyyyyyyy
and, when her brother visited, he said
that her English sounded like my Welsh.

Ramla could roll her hips like a Goddess.
She had lips you should and shouldn't fuck with
and a spare prayer mat,
and she'd say "Come, Allah is waiting to hold space."

Ramla's arms were everything,
and the bird song would signal
that we'd survived another night
and she'd say
"They are carrying everything you've ever lost
home."

3

I was always all up in Cee's business
his reluctance made my game long.

But he'd slide by, hood up, eyes wide, tone deep
"Mufasaaa."

I'd be 10% giggle, 20% block up,
the rest maintaining gangsta.

I was always all up in Cee's business;
slowly we got closer.

Often he'd just internal chest laugh;
sometimes he'd be defeated and smile.

Then came the imitation
and I learned that I say the word 'like' like all the time
and I had a lilt
that he learnt to like, like.

I was always all up in Cee's business:
tea time, 3am,
had my own knock
and he'd unlock
sometimes with, sometimes without eye contact
and I'd help myself to his toiletries.
Hell! He eventually let me wear his FUBU, his hoods,
which was ridiculous
cos he was big and wore even bigger
and I was tiny, wearing huge.

I was always all up in Cee's business;
he eventually started telling me stories
about his Daddy, how he looked just like him,
stories about Nigeria and London,
how both were home.

I was always all up in Cee's business;
he didn't have much choice teaching me to MC,
and, on nights when my demons were dancing darkness,
he'd sing me Jill Scott lullabies until I found sleep.

4

Irish Paula had complex issues –
that's why I loved her.
She could read your religion
and would remember exactly fuck-all like me.

Irish Paula was the friend
that hooked out condoms,
located lost tampons
and would never tell tales.

We both carried the cross,
drank Southern Comfort and lemonade.
She blistered every finger sealing my braids
and fluffing-up hash, road trippin' the real landscapes

Mainly industrial,
the sexy stench of steel passing Port Talbot
Operation 9 bar from The West,
intentions of profit but we hot-box the block.

We watch episodes of *Shameless*
on repeat,
stop believing in Johnny.
We now pray for a Steve.

Irish Paula adds blisters to those blisters

We've got complex issues,
that's why we're sisters.

5

Julia, from Newcastle
(We call her Queen)
will become my very best friend ever, forever --
the first girl I meet
who's got Daddy Issues just like me.

I make it my business
to fuck up all the bad boys that fuck with her
and she breaks the spell,
meets a Welsh King.

But I'll make many mistakes,
over and over again.
I will learn that Daddy Issues
is a gaslit blanket
that gives predators permission to treat you badly.

But even those kind of contracts have an expiry
and she'll be there,
waiting for me at the homecoming
when the war is over.

Marley Brando

I'd never quite felt anything like it –

pains in my chest
sickness
battery-flavoured breath
cold compress…

I held him
begging
by a radiator to warm him
sobbing

My whispered wishes will to wake…

avail-unavailable
I placed him on his gold and black-velvet throne
disbelief driven
for communal comprehension

stood around like loyal Hells Angels
drunk on pride
whispering willing wishes
to the leader of the pack.

Uncle Gwyn

He had all the weekend papers
the ones with the magazines
I'd rummage and ravage
cutting out future dreams

rescuing images
icons
false idols
slivers of spells.

His R's made me royal
His D's looked Chinese
His G's arresting
His V's gothic feel

Who taught him to write?
Who gave him his hand?
The eldest child of the Davies tribe
my style carries these DNA strands

As I scribe this almost-lost-dynasty
with only memory
I should have been there properly
when yours was failing you.

Uncle John

1

Carbonised crystal
dense trench pension

packed tight and tidy
the occasional rumbling conversation

when disturbed by a hand
or a back, a shovel

adding from sacks
or in-to-tin buckets.

Foolish frogs squat
shaft drop on timers

unpredictable nature
unforgiving thunder

tarmac tongue
caked caps and tips

learning the old ways
from his eyes and song.

2

He was ashamed
of his handwriting
but he taught me
to use a pen

blue Bic biro
transparent body
drawing ravens and trees
houses with chimneys

pipe smoking men
wearing cowboy hats
big smiles, wide eyed
shaded jawlines.

He was ashamed
of his handwriting
but he carried
a betting mini

in his jacket top pocket
road ready
he'd judge on stats or guts
I'd choose by colour

Grand National tradition
I'd forgot about 'til now
purple and yellow in honour
you said hi with a prize.

I took a baby blue betting Bic
as a reminder
of the spells you taught me
jousting, fencing – precursor calligraphy.

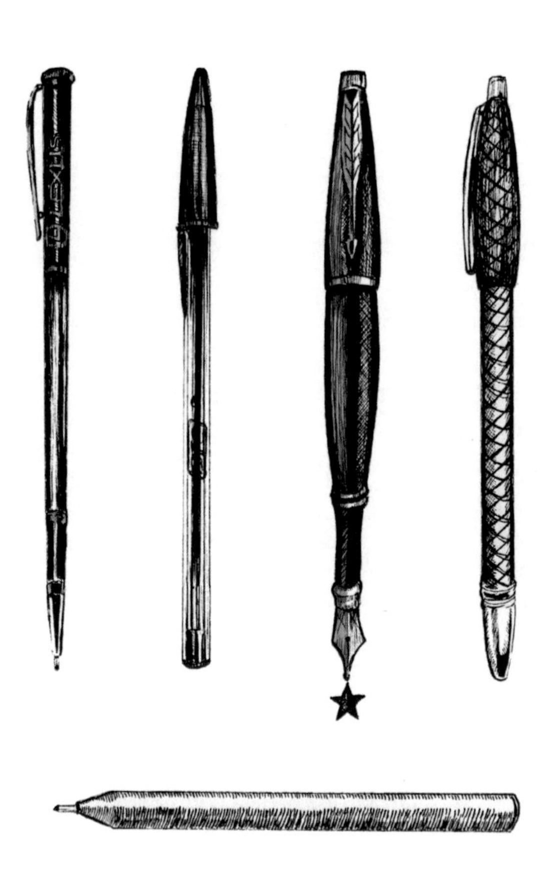

Llanelli

Tammy Girl trips for new disco rigout
Made cushions from the dresses I outgrew
Pieces of the past that softly furnish

Charity shop in its place and next door
Once little store of jewels and trinkets
Tammy girl trips for new disco rigout

Silver jade treasure still got today safe
Market filled with every elder I've lost
Pieces of the past that softly furnish

Found in solstice wreaths of remembrance
Glossy leaves glimmer guilt of forgetting
Tammy girl trips for new disco rigout

I lost the tribe's maps to sacred spaces
Did not save any of the coins they gave
Pieces of the past that softly furnish

Flood gates centre stage stood in aged arcade
Laced in Phyllis' Amami embrace
Tammy Girl trips for new disco rigout
Pieces of the past that softly furnish.

Battle Rapper in the Boardroom

1

She says my words are black
She likes to keep things white
She has Shhhh! in her backstory
So she thinks this makes her right.

She has a black-list
Sword on standby
"Fetch the cheese board
for her inner toad,"

that keeps the Kingdom.
Don't defy Dylan's Duchess.
I'm the trapped trauma of my tribe:
2nd class stamp this S.O.S.

Allowed in her courtyard
If offering up ribs,
I make arrows from refrain
with Ink Caps that can't forgive.

2

This week I learnt critique
from masters that don't leave feedback sheets

I seek CPD on the daily
and my home needs me

whitewash operation thriving
but I'm a blagger without blinkers

literary activism happens with refrain
and tears carry keys if you taste them.

3

They cut out her throat
her tongue wasn't enough

they rationed her ink
black-list-spilled guts

they tarnished her skill
they soiled her song

didn't need money
just liked sourcing souls

but hers has a blue egg
placed there by a witch

when magpies spy shine
the crows congregate

dogs know she sees them
Kash Koolidge schooled

dysfunctional prenups
but she speaks and seeks truth.

4

Radical clique bypassing gate keepers
take our communities back to campfires

you are obstructing my view of the universe
one foot on the pavement, pen ready

cliché can't predict the weather
but you can't control it either

so let the spirits dance
in this strangled prose of a hybrid.

Bali Mynah

My people were a stocky sort
both sexes big breasted
their tips tattooed black.

My people loved the rain
raised me to nurse
raised both sexes to service the nest.

My people's dialects change rapidly with distance
we learn more when our call types are different.

My people sing old hymns with new hearts
but we are worth more to you caged.

Trips to the Underworld

There are digital borders between us
screaming freedom and fairness
promoting political awareness.

There are digital borders between us
that keep us absent from the present moment
form the moment we open our eyes and rise.

There are digital borders between us
and your smile
lies well.

There are digital borders
com-part-ment-alising
us-into-camps

well-lit zebra crossings
inviting, alluring
but don't dare step outside the borders.

You can admire the horizon
briefly
before we remind you of the borders

we'll put gaps in the fence
we love bloody knees
and purple bruises

With confidence and privilege come clashes
don't get ideas above your station
we were just ticking boxes.

Cravings and Longing
(lullabies from Y Gegin Fach)

Belly Big, I sat by the kitchen sink
Comforted by redundant shoe polish
Licking the Brasso lid – torments to swig.

Every Friday you'd scrub off the week's stains
Fingertips unscathed, old newspaper way
Belly Big, I sat by the kitchen sink.

I'd watch you speak the languages of crows
How I'd take back all the shoes I've outgrown
Licking the Brasso lid – torments to swig.

Furious sun kissed forearms, your shoulders pale
Left not a speck on your winter white vest
Belly Big, I sat by the kitchen sink.

Every bit of gold gleamed on Saturdays
Ironised insight, rustic flare filled space
Licking the Brasso lid – torments to swig.

So sure of your chores, made them pride of place
Your every flash of me was centre stage
Belly Big, I sat by the kitchen sink
Licking the Brasso lid, torments to swig.

Birth Plan

I wish you could sail our seas
for a whole year and not see
us.
We use our senses in the darkness,
finely tuned (in)to one another's scents;
a sureness in this ocean, our Planet B.

T H I C K layers of blubber ensures
we both survive the harshness of winter
and in the vastness; nesting is simplified
in this meditative slow and steady drive
to the calm of the equator

where we birth; storm and cold weathers can't hurt
and you only see the surface of this world
for your first breath before you journey
for hyper-immune mammary cream.

You feed and feed freely; we are not public property.

We return to polar seas and feast.
By autumn you leave,
learning to embrace
solidarity.
The colder our depths, the harder our hum
                                                  h u m m
                                                   h u m m m travels
so we will never truly be apart.

Sometimes it is beautiful
to be hard to
                  find.

Midwives are the worst gardeners

I was nesting furiously inside
while he cleared the land
his bare back to the sun

strimmer in hand
petrol fumed air
making things right

his face white with shock
when he found her
near-miss trauma

of guts in the gully
of guilt in his eyes
but I've got too much on my mind

to care properly
if we feed her she'll stay
my mother says she'll smother

or knock over the basket
or carry disease
I can't take the risk

but he insists on an offering
for the almost crime scene
with concerns she's not moved.

We find her tortoise shell stillness
surrendered to duty
and I surrender to mine

she must be hungry
she is their feast
my shame fills her bowl.

I birth with tears and tears
with scars you can't see
baby won't latch

midwives are the worst gardeners
say baby is a fractious lip sucker
stop this nonsense, mix up formula.

Tortoise shell teacher
help me surrender to duty
because all our babies are made of milk.

We are in the fourth trimester

and it appears that we only want to talk
if we like the conversation.
Keep your distress signals faint, quaint, quirky
and fit in with our plans, stick to a rota.

We are in the fourth trimester
and have a rigorous Instagram schedule,
objectification disguised as pride, flash in eyes
and we'd rather you played along,
especially at night.

We are in the fourth trimester
and I'm doing it our way, keeping you close,
away from the sharpness of winter and tongues,
sinking in the language of your star,
relearning my ancestral song.

We are in the fourth trimester
chest to chest
my heart beat your first drum
the only rhythm and routine
you know.

Itsa Girl!

At the news of my first baby, my Cockney Step-Nan, Nanny Lil, and her best friend Big Brenda got right to work; lashings of lush yellows, lamb like whites, and the most beautiful bounty of booties. I always imagined myself as someone that would not want to find out the sex of the baby, but Nanny Lil and Big Brenda were waiting in the wings, wanting, and NEEDING to know what colour was next! The news of a girl made her world! I think she almost forgot she was grieving for Grandad, who had recently passed over, and in honesty, she had waited her whole life for this moment, for the news of a girl. She was blessed with two boys, both she was expecting to be girls, and adamant they would and should be, and the initial shock really threw her. She was in so much denial that she dressed them in fabulous frills for the first few weeks.
"A girl! A girl!" she screamed, and through the phone I could hear the ground beneath her rumble. She really was jumping for joy. There is something about the promise of pink wool that makes some elderly women totally bat-shit crazy.
Nanny Lil died shortly after my baby girl's birth. I couldn't part with the clothes, so many unworn, due to the sheer abundance and a freak heatwave. I really missed her during my second pregnancy. But she was there, at the gender scan, jumping for joy in my mind's eye, "It's a girl, a girl!" I'm sure she knew all along! Her and Big Brenda made enough knits for all my unborn children. My girls were gifted with her last words, of love and comfort, security and warmth.

Itsa Worry!

They have unresolved
issues that weren't
then

no Lexis
inkless pen
then

skip me glossary
men were men
then

weak with freak
I see
them

hashtagless era
feds non-believers
then

impregnated
segregated
faint-fetters

third generation
shape-shifting
maybe

my daughters will be free.

Toby said

#metoo is a fashion
I suck in my face, breathe,
try to be equal opportunity freedom of expression.
I say "Toby, bro, can you elaborate on that one?"

He explains how women wear it as a badge to VIP events:
a girls' club hijacking propaganda of effects
for a bit more spotlight at red carpet pretence,
a poor me-pity-party firing that causes masculinity dents…

If #metoo is a fashion it was tailored to fit me.
It clings to my skin and it feels proper itchy.
There's too many fake, filled-in pockets
And the overfill landslides inside me.
#I'm 10 – in the corridor of Primary.
#I'm 12 – the taxi driver likes to flash me.
#I'm 15 and my friend said he'd walk me home safely.
#I'm every 5 star holiday delicacy.

#I'm 9 – the scuba-diving teacher in the light of day.

#I'm 14 tricked with the promise of baby turtles.
#I didn't know shit like that happened.

#I'm primed, road ready, my boss' brother lets me pretend I'm helping him with the stock room.
#but he owns his own nightclub and I'm underage; I'm learning female currency.
#I later tell my boss, who later turns my own sister against me:
they fill her head with images not true, tell her I'm a druggie.
#they tell anyone who'll listen that I'm a druggie.
HASHTAG I'm 15 – CC forcefully behind the long distance lorries...

#I fell in love with a bad boy.
#I was used to his behaviours.
#I've still got lumps on my skull from when my father threw me against cookers and radiators.
I say threw, but a single slap across my face could do it.
His girlfriend watched smirking, like I was his ex-girlfriend, not a child, assaulted in her own home, without the words to call it out.
#I'm 24 and in love with an artist who breaks me and my ribs.
If I go to the police, he's my boyfriend, they'll think I'm crazy
Like the times I've called the cops as a child "Come quick!
I think my Dadi might kill my Mami."
And the cops rock up, and the men rest on the window ledge talking tax
because businessmen never seem to end up in custody,
especially not in the 80s

#I'm 26 and I'm in love with a rapper, who one day loses his shit,
his reason being is because I can't articulate myself properly.
He roughs me up and the force of my face fighting the floor chips at least 3 teeth
and he says "You need help! You need professional help!"
And he was right, so right, back then I didn't know what gas-lighting meant
Even though I'd lived it, and wore its scent
And there's so much more denial, because I still blame myself;
And there is so much more that I've not listed, because my brain is on the defence.
HASHTAG I've got cubs to protect: first degree tears, stitches fresh.

But one day, on some random day: BANG. Epiphany!
Flashback, random meeting, picking up groceries,
Gut feeling: BANG. That's what that was,
because we are all learning this new vocabulary, collectively.
We are digging up demons, trapped trauma, dis-ease
So if #metoo is a fashion, then I'm the mother-fuckin'-fashion police,
and YOU didn't follow the dress code.

Koala Mufasa

My daughter talks to all the flowers
and all the insects like she knows them.
She finds paths I can't quite see
and I lose logistics squeezing through

into other worlds where crows are the same size as children
and trees house entire communities,
ten generations of forest fairies
and all the sacred secrets of the universe…

My daughter stops to smell everything –
the leaves, the breeze, my ancestors' memories,
with an insight and understanding that pre-dates me
and her arms have all the answers.

My daughter laughs hysterically in her dreams,
wakes kissing me, "Good morning, Mami,"
puts on sunglasses and dances
to the invisible beats of spiritual masters.

Babymoon

Good morning Mr Tree.
I'm so glad that I forgot
to pull down
the bamboo blinds last night

to be greeted with the whiteness
of the morning light
that really highlights
your deep-brown perfection thirsty for spring

your sturdy stature
your thickness
your sureness
your info-structure

your origami grandness
botanical bonsai high in the sky
babe and I stare hypnotised
watching the wind work

through your bare broccoli like branches
sending your sage waves
babe ripples right back
to you and the birds checking in

to the finest skyscraper
in this skyline of simplicity
perfectly fitting on this backdrop
of wetness this Wednesday

and you, my Teeny Tiny Turtle, look perfect
in your white vest of clouds
that says "having a lazy day"
augmenting your olive skin

your mahogany-velvet hair
your mild eyes that I get lost in
your button nose poetry
your ears that belong to fairies

we are truly
loaded with wonder
taught by the wisest of trees
that are so evidently

watching over us
and they are just as pleased that we
forgot to pull down
the bamboo blinds last night

Here

In this space, it is both lovely and
lonely.
I spend my everymomentinawhirlwindofchores and never-ever
stop doing laundry
but the basket is never-ever empty.

In this space, I sometimes must choose
who to love.

Third attempt at nursing one to sleep
and the other throws a fluorescent green
bubble mix bottle
and I snatch it and throw it across the room
and now we are all crying in chorus.

I take extra-long drying my hair just to enjoy the silence then
it's right back to business
and I spend an eternity going 'round and 'round in circles
picking things up for you to just
throw
picking things up but still always tripping
over
and I wipe down the grime of this town, this Wild West where
I am a wench for you all to quench
your thirsts
and she screams "I want" while I'm with baby in arms and
I remind her of manners
remind her I am not a slave, I am mother and
I realise that these are the exact same thing.

So let me rest a moment and I'll be fine with that, in this
space
both lovely and
lonely.

You are six months old today my love

and there is an ocean between us.

If could dive in and swim I would.
My arms feel useless
my breasts don't know what to do…

I've been munched on by mosquitoes
I had your milk
I wish I had you.

You are six months old today my love
and I am in Finland.
The last time I was here was with you
just us two

visiting galleries, patisseries
train rides, parks, gigs after dark
belly big and dreams even bigger
and that time I cried for your big sister

at Kiasma
us connecting to space
us swimming in art

You are kind of like that now
you like to look about
like everything is
an exhibition.

When you were weeks old
I took you to see
Marion Cheung's
Lost Connections.

In the café that day
so many women stopped to say
how beautiful, how forward
how sweet, how proud

You are six months old today my love
I wanted to visit our Kiasma
but it was closed
so I walked the streets;

the heavy scent of lavender led me
to an art gallery
where I met
a Finnish version of Nain.

Red lipstick her signature
classy and quirky
just like my mother.

She told me about the old piece of furniture
the heavy use of lavender
just like my mother.

Trying to get rid of tan lines
in time for the exhibition
just like my mother.

Reapplying red lipstick for a photo
no mirror
just like my mother.

Marilyn Monroe – just like my mother
the lavender, reconnects me to my mother
who is caring for you both for me to be here.

You are six months old today my love
I'm sat alone in a sauna crying buckets
of love, of "I don't know what."

I can see clearly, the day you were born
how far we've come,
sat in a sauna, mothering myself.

Schooled by a Sunflower

You can't see that rainbow?
free from black and white
free from fight
free for all

I've got a Robin that wants to move in
and I'm on first name terms with our resident Seagull
and we live on a mountain
so what does that tell you?

Last week I got schooled by a Sunflower!
All the others at the end of season
this little one branched from a stem
has been bashed about and drenched

hell the winds took out trees
but that little Sunflower
the still-standing slow-starter
watching the skies

waiting to see
the rainbow
with
me.

Bus Stop Bitches

It was her spot, her tiny place of understanding, with a royal blue backdrop, against her Mr Haul duffle style coat that "Nain got for me." It was her spot, and even if someone was stood in that spot she'd shuffle them over. What changed? We went away for a few days, and she was un-welcomed back with spies, waiting, watching as she approached, and they'd position themselves – in her spot.
She cried, pleading with a woman, a mother of an older boy, explaining "that's my spot," and they snubbed her. She doesn't understand snubbed yet, so I take the bullet, but we both know it's wrong, and so does the boy, the woman's son, and he's moved. But this woman, this mother, is having a stand-off with a 3-year-old over a spot at the bus stop, in a bus stop big enough for everybody to stand up against the royal blue backdrop. There's even enough room on the wall right opposite for everyone to take a seat.
Getting ready for the next day at the bus stop I say "Koala, shall we stand somewhere else at the bus stop today?"
"No Mami," she says, starting to cry, "I want to stand in my spot!"
She doesn't understand why it's such a big deal.
"OK."
I don't think anybody should be underestimating me. I've just dressed and fed two children in less than half an hour and we're out the door...
We are within their range. The shuffling about of bodies starts. Woman/mother, ten times the size of my daughter, stands, in her spot. We reach the bus stop. Koala, tiny Koala stands in front of woman/mother, looks all the way up to her face, looks her right in the eye with the saddest, most sincere 3-year-old plea, "that's my spot".
Woman/mother looks me right in the eye, that pierces "I don't give a fuck," with a smirking silence that screams "someone needs to school her – who does she think she is?"

I, Woman, Koala's Mother, look her dead in the eye right back, but I'm not smirking, my lips are moving…
"Koala doesn't sleep well most nights. Koala cries most mornings before school. This spot is her TINY way of working out the world."
Wide eyed woman/mother finally replies "Okayyyyy. All riiiite!!!" shuffle shuffle – silence...
Dead silence.
My right eye on Turtle in the pram next to us, my left eye on my thumb, doing circular smoothing motions on Koala's right hand, Koala stood – in her spot.
Still silence…
broken by the biggest bullshit small talk of knock-off gear bouncing about the estate, vape juice, kids fighting over phones and games, mother/woman smacks her son about something to do with the phone, and I'm just waiting for the rumble of the green bus, kissing Koala saying "I love you," over and over, before putting her on the bus, then trying to find her seat from the outside, which is very difficult because she's so small, her head doesn't quite reach the window, but I always wave anyway. The bus pulls off and I walk away with Turtle, whose pram I keep stopping to kiss her head, holding back tears, sucking them deep down, not because I'm upset over woman/mother, not for myself, but I'm furious that woman/mother thinks she can bully my baby. I'm furious that that woman/mother thinks this is about my daughter. All this says so much more about her than it does about my daughter. How mother/woman must be so lost in this world that she still needs a spot at the bust stop, keeping a 3-year-old in her place in the process. I'm furious that my children will have to experience this and more, for decades before they have the real understanding, a vocabulary to call it out. I'm furious that these parents are a reminder of what school is like. I send my girl, my precious girl, into a jungle every day, armed only with her heart on her sleeve and a snack box, and a change of clothes in-case she has an accident. Armed only with what she knows to date

against people whose parents think it's OK to bully a 3-year-old in her own bus stop, against people who have had years to master emotional guerrilla warfare to spit spite in such a way you can't see it, yet, but will, she will and she must call it out. When I called my father out, when I'd learnt how to articulate all the things I could not grasp when things were so much different (or are they?)... when marital rape wasn't illegal, when men owned their women and children, when children should be seen and not heard, when you didn't understand how much you looked like your mother (but his girlfriend did), when you didn't understand gas-lighting even when you looked it up, when you didn't have cuts and bruises to prove it but you had tonsillitis over and over and over again, tonsils scarred by the severity, antibiotic immunity, life threatening fevers, sweat drenched bedding, hallucinations beyond comprehension, then and now, ...My father said "What's in the past is in the past... you can't keep looking in your rear view mirrors, you'll crash." He'd say this, left eye twitching, an uncontrollable nervous twitch, a gift, from his mother. Years of abuse, a woman/mother he never forgave, never mentioned, and you thought you might die if you ever did.
Gas-lighting, all of it, and when you learn to read it, you can't un-see it. But gas-lighters forget that you helped them write the rule book, and if you survive enough explosions, you learn that your legs are for running.
My father said "if you don't like what people do, or what they represent, you don't quarrel with them, you just dismiss them".
I haven't seen my father in over a decade.
I have to go back to the bus stop, on my own. Woman/mother is not there, but her friends are, and they've been talking. I sit right next to them. One gives me a sour puss "Allrite," the other, an awkward "Hiaaa," (she wasn't there this morning, but she's heard). They talk bullshit about sunbeds, vapes, coils (contraceptive coils or vape pen coils, I'm not sure, who cares), underactive thyroids... (Penguin, that's my name for her, well, she likes to diagnose people, because there isn't a member of

her family that doesn't have something wrong with them that's wrong with someone else)... the local doctors' surgery being closed on Thursdays...they just talk and talk…
"I goes to Rhydfelin if I cants gets to Ponty, it's easier than Dewi Sant, and I just buzzes her into my Bampy's flat without 'avin to go in the building, and e's first floor so he can manage thaaa, and she just pushes his wheelchair back in, see," and they talk, ignore me, talk, vape, talk, vape, vape...
Woman/mother's partner rocks up. Vape vape vape.
Woman/mother's sister rocks up. Everyone just carries on ignoring me, thank fuck, cos I'd have fuck all to contribute to this conversation other than
"Owww, you might not have thyroid issues, like Professor Penguin here is suggesting. Your constant migraines and eye infection might have something to do with your excessive sunbed sessions".
The green bus rocks up. Everyone, and I mean everyone's children gets off the bus crying.
They've all been fighting...One, two, three, four,
My Koala – she's beaming!
"Mamiiii!"
I thank the bus lady and bus driver, who say she's been fab, and she told them she was hoping it was me picking her up today. We kiss. We hug. I do her coat zip up and see her seren gwyrdd, and her pockets full of daises "for you Mami". We kiss. We hug. We really stop at the bus stop, and she says "I love you Mami."
I love you too Koala Mufasa, I really, truly do.

Insight

You called me Dadi
knowing I wasn't.
I wondered if that
was your way of saying
I work too much.

You sat next to me with
your scissors, red, mine black.
You cut up the revolution
with a precision I'd taught you
then you asked me to dance.

Nameless Love

You left me
At approximately ten past three;
I thought you'd stay

at least another day.

Purged, made a big plop
Red Sea filled pan
No hope of rescue
Romanticised I'd find you
To tuck you into a trinket
To cradle or bury proper…

My womb raged until the morning
He got Koala ready for school
I really needed to hug her
For me more
But stage 2 ambushed
Set me in paralysis at the top of the stairs
I shout "Have a good day sweetheart."
She blows me cute kisses
I hold on until she's out of site
Underrated the urgent onset
Rivers running down my legs
A fist full of jelly falls
when I pull down my knickers
Thuds the white lino
Splatters the walls and leaves foot prints
Stranded, no toilet roll or wet wipes
Men half shop
No time to be pissed off
But I'm so bloody pissed off
The shower amplifies my shame
Wrap myself in a towel

Look for rags under the sink
Find some old stained outgrown baby grows
Douse the crime scene in bleach
Before anyone can see

I'm so sorry I did this to your memory
We both deserved better
I pray that Nanna was there to meet you
And that her realm makes more sense.

In loving memory of Doll

My Nanna's sister Dorothy
spent her life in/as a photo
sat on top of a posh teak retro cabinet
gold frame setting her huge thick waves.

They called her Doll
my hair is just like hers
the only kind you'll find
on my Mami's side.

Her dainty features carry a sureness
her non-smile a non-conforming protest
she could have been a secret agent
passing around underground information.

She just hung there in the background
you could feel her in every room
I saw her in Nanna's every tear
Forever 24. Forever Nanna's Doll.

I always asked questions
especially about photos
Nanna would always answer
maybe deep down she knew I was undercover too.

"She died from septicaemia;
bled to death from an illegal abortion."

And it's like you know and don't know
how big this all is
but you know Doll was too beautiful
to die of anything.

Nanna never forgot
of how her family ignored her cries
too late alarming the Doctor
Nanna held her hand as she died.

With every glance of the photo
you try to fix this, try to understand
It took three generations to tell Doll's story
and I wish I had my Nanna's hand.

Nanna's Hands

Honeysuckle, snowdrops, cowboy movies,
Her hard work broke every finger both hands;
Her hands that rubbed warmth back into my feet.

Kept chickens for eggs and could break their necks
Without sweat, her Sunday dinners the best,
Honeysuckle, snowdrops, cowboy movies.

Could wire-wool tiled floors until they looked new,
Power polished shoes that reflect right back
Her hands that rubbed warmth back into my feet.

Up at six to light fires for family,
Never stopped knitting, always outstretched arms,
Honeysuckle, snowdrops, cowboy movies.

Never sick, but dementia became her
Shifted tons of coal, hand washed clothes old school
Her hands that rubbed warmth back into my feet.

Magical pantry, potent poultice paste,
Strong hands on my hair, tells me pride will pinch.
Honeysuckle, snowdrops, cowboy movies,
Her hands that rubbed warmth back into my feet.

I thought of Helen today

by my side that time
I was having secrets
removed.

She taught me kindness,
art and valleys.
We later fell out
over boys and money.

I thought of Helen today,
of how she stayed
the whole time
holding my hand.

Gone

At home, I just needed bed.
I read *Grief is the Thing with Feathers* in one sitting.
I cry I love you I love you I love you into my pillow
Trying to erase ever imagining your name
Your sex
Your face.

A positive test is all I have left
Hidden in a box
Inside a drawer
Hidden
Hidden.

I pack up the pram
That Turtle has only just outgrown.
The car seat and the crib are immaculate
The main seat needs a scrub.

Turtle plays with her baby doll for hours
Imagining she's mother, big sister, imagining…
Claims the car seat in protest
Forces me to imagine too
But I want so much real with her
My getting bigger girl, still my baby.

Mr Imam, I heard you calling

...night after night.

Mr Imam, night after night
you broke the morning's brief silent stillness.

Mr Imam, there's a conflict
between the calling of the party and your temple.

Mr Imam, I chose you
your women dressed me in robes of royal blue.

Mr Imam, I joined them
I followed their every breath, bend and bow.

Mr Imam, I made my body streamline
I'm used to the surrender.

Mr Imam, I found faith when I was five
but the big guy's door wasn't always open.

Mr Imam, I shouldn't be here 'cos I'm bleeding
but I've had bigger blood baths than this.

Mr Imam, I watched your men in rows
'Do they pray for us?'

Mr Imam, you held my hand
but I wish you'd held me.

Mr Imam, my heart is broken.
Maybe you know.

I pray you call me again.

What we did to Solstice

guilt-hostility-guilt-gurn-belt
my womb and lips
red raw flag way beyond surrender

senseless drones and clones
desperate for
this!?!

once upon a time made sense once
safeguarded 'till the darkness lifted

I'll do better next year
cut cords with this catalogue culture
imposed on me with hostility

disguised as pride and security
in payday-chains-when-really-pay-day-is-the-rain
but we can't keep our waters clean

Now the darkness sits in
picking at the ribs of our own ruin
I wish never that for them

be makers, never buyers
in this land of soiled harvests
where the tribes are manner-less-mice growing limbs
for unnaturally selected kings.

Braiding Sweetgrass with Uncle John

He taught me to braid Sweetgrass
so delicately that my fingertips
now write poetry in my daughter's hair.

He taught me that we are a circle
with a shared language of gratitude
and harvests should always be honourable

but everything for sale here is dead.
Showers no longer bring flowers
and all the medicine is missing.

Teach our children to forage furiously
with reciprocity, then there'll never be
a shortfall.

Let them show you mystical symbols-
do not tarnish their respect for ravens
and instinctiveness to smell flowers.

I teach my daughters to braid Sweetgrass
to remind us of how
the world is meant to be.

Fire People

We,
learnt to take it back to the fire.
We remembered that poetry, music and dance are the same strand of DNA that is present in everything,
our fire within...

We, learnt to respect those that chose
to come here from the clouds,
stepped up, chose the pain of our poisons,
and their connection to the land
blew our understanding out of the water.

They, worked like ants in the toxic soils...
They charmed the birds from the trees
then in turn the birds shifted seeds
and those seeds grew fruits and flowers, bushes and berries
and more birds came, more ants worked, and our ancestors the trees
both above and
below
reshaped this landscape, instigated the impossible
by command of the Fire People.

The prophecy of our Rainbow Children is true.

Trigger Warnings

1

My baby girl getting bigger now
reminds me that she's almost 5
every time we Skype
she asks will I be back in time?

My baby girl getting bigger now
whose sports day I missed
heard she broke the rules
deliberately ran the wrong way, twice.

My baby girl getting bigger now
made touchdown just like the movies
despite classic zero-to-prick-quick
and my other baby strapped-in-off-limits.

My baby girl getting bigger now
gets her first lesson in slut-shaming

I vow to make this my last...

2

I vow to make this my last
on the way to the airport car park
hijacked by Swedish cranes
and they say

you passed through Nothing to Declare too apace
take us
as your totem
take your past
use it to strengthen your present
keep your own council
trust that we will protect
balance will be

"But you are monogamy?"

take your past
use it to strengthen your present
find a freedom programme
face a fresh fight
but know
that the weigh-in is dirty
that from the first round
the referee will be blind

"So is it not safer to stay?"

take your past
use it
all your triggers make you a gun
we are justice
we are Satan's enemies
we carry prayers to the heavens
we will walk you home...

3

We will walk you home too
say the hummingbirds
travellers of vast distances
masters of the present and backwards
territorial protection
messengers between the gods and ancestors
symbol of infinity they feast on life's sweet nectars
honouring small joys, letting go of the toxic
and they've removed all the sunflowers from the garden
and replaced them with wild-woman-magik
violet bells that wave without wind
and my big girl getting bigger says
"Can you hear them Mami, they are screaming for you,"
and my Nanna is sat waiting, making poultice for my wounds.

NOTES

Page 19: ***Y Gegin Fach***

This poem is bilingual. My family were fluent Welsh speakers but, historically, my family and other Welsh families were made to feel that their native language was inadequate, simple and wrong. They were taught that English was the language of advancement. Consequently, my family thought they were hindering my development by speaking the Welsh language. However, it was always there in the background. My peoples' Welsh is beautiful, and I want to honour this.

Y gegin fach: little kitchen / back room / working quarters of the home.
Cwtch dan stâr: cupboard under the stairs. I still remember the smell of it.
Papur wal: wallpaper
Cadair ffyddlon Auntie Phyllis: Auntie Phyllis' faithful chair.
yn croeshawu hi nôl pob nos Wener: welcoming her home every Friday night (after a busy day shopping).
Clincian y llwy yn erbyn y gwydr: clinking of the spoon against the glass.
basn llawn bara-the: basin full of tea bread (*bara-the* is an old, maintained custom from war time, of bread broken up into bits in a bowl and drenched in strong, black tea).
Y bwrdd cadarn: strong, solid table
Caer: fortress
Papur: paper
Duw: God, as in "good God/well I never"
Sâm: lard
Bosh: a very local Welsh word for sink – I grew up watching men and women use it equally.

Page 21: ***Juniors***

Cymraeg y ddaear: Native, colloquial Welsh for that specific region of Wales.

Cwtchy: Cuddly

Page 41: ***Tina, the Staffordshire Bull Terrier***

baller: a person who starts out with nothing and makes it to the top.

Page 77: ***Bus Stop Bitches***

Mr Haul: Mr Sun

Seren Gwyrdd: Green Star

Page 91: ***Braiding Sweetgrass with Uncle John***

Poem inspired by Robin Wall Kimmerer's *Braiding Sweetgrass.*

Indigo Dreams Publishing Ltd
24, Forest Houses
Cookworthy Moor
Halwill
Beaworthy
Devon
EX21 5UU
www.indigodreams.co.uk